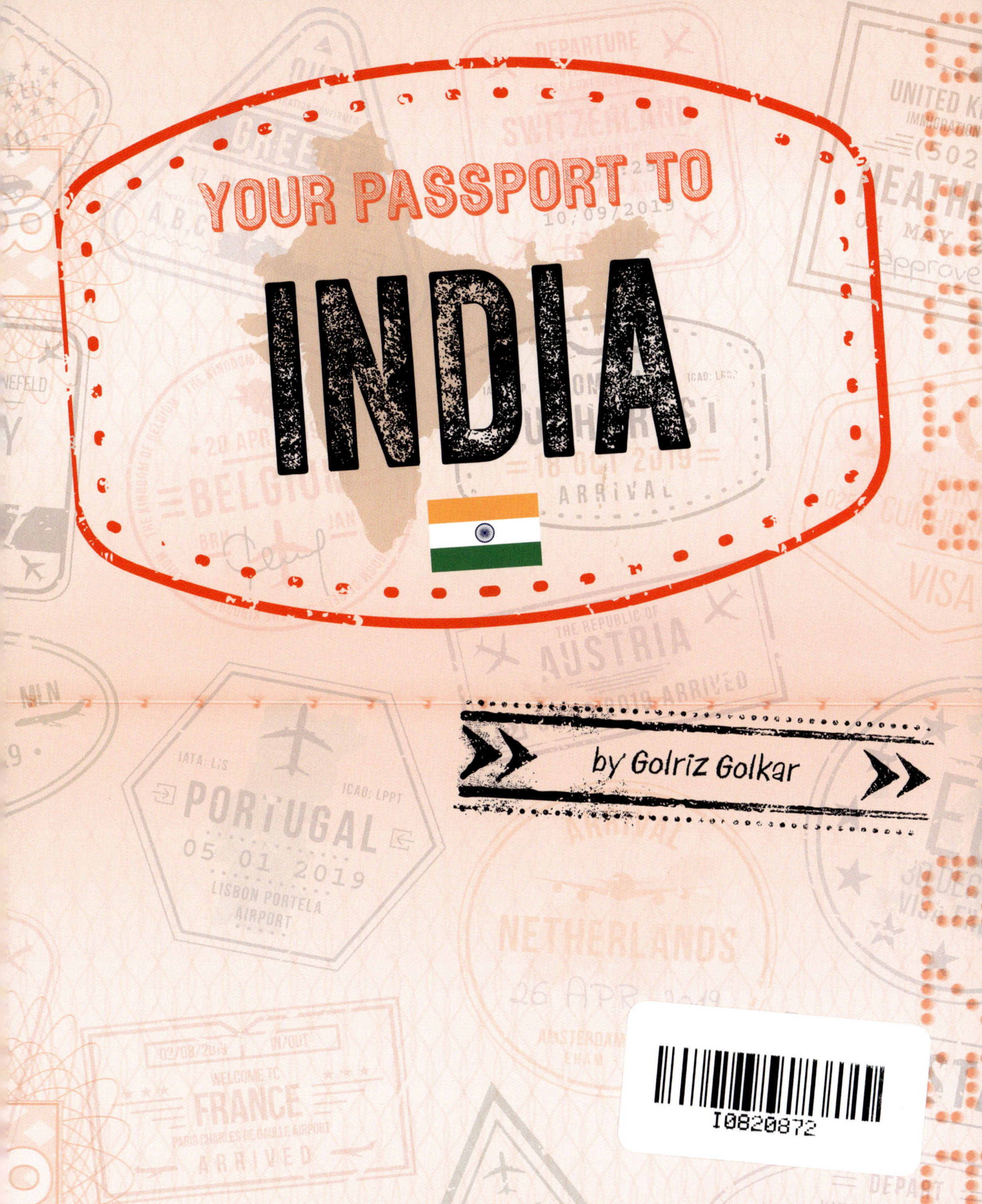

YOUR PASSPORT TO INDIA

by Golriz Golkar

CAPSTONE PRESS
a capstone imprint

Published by Capstone Press, an imprint of Capstone
1710 Roe Crest Drive, North Mankato, Minnesota 56003
capstonepub.com

Library of Congress Cataloging-in-Publication Data is available on the Library of Congress website.
ISBN: 9798875245718 (hardcover)
ISBN: 9798875245664 (paperback)
ISBN: 9798875245671 (ebook PDF)

Summary: What is it like to live in or visit India? What makes India's culture unique? Explore the sights and daily lives of Indians.

Editorial Credits
Editor: Elaine Duncan; Designer: Sarah Bennett; Media Researcher: Rebekah Hubstenberger; Production Specialist: Tori Abraham

Image Credits
Capstone: Eric Gohl, 5; Getty Images: - /AFP, 9, Abhishek Chinnappa, 19 (top left), Charles Bowman/robertharding, 15, hadynyah, 24, iStock/RavindraJoisa, 16, iStock/Ravsky, 22, iStock/Roop_Dey, front cover, Mayur Kakade, 20, narvikk, 7, sabirmallick, 14, Surjeet Yadav, 28; Shutterstock: AbhishekMittal, 27, Boris Stroujko, 18, David Bokuchava, 21, Finn stock, 6, PradeepGaurs, 19 (top right), saiko3p, 17 (top), Shutter by M, 17 (bottom right); Superstock/IMAGO/had fotos, 11

Design Elements
Getty Images: iStock/Yevhenii Dubinko; Shutterstock: charnsitr, Flipser, Net Vector, pingebat, Rhealea

Printed and bound in Malaysia. 006460

CONTENTS

Words in **bold** are in the glossary.

CHAPTER ONE

WELCOME TO INDIA!

The sun rises in the city of Jaipur, India. It casts a glow against pink buildings. Visitors stroll past the Hawa Mahal in the historic center. The building has many honeycomb windows.

Next door, they visit the galleries of the City Palace. They admire many royal costumes and paintings. At the Tripolia Bazar, they buy colorful fabrics, jewelry, and rugs. The aroma of fried onion pastries drifts from street sellers nearby. India is an ancient land where the traditions of many **cultures** thrive together.

AN ANCIENT COUNTRY

India is a country in Asia. Most of its land is surrounded by water. The Arabian Sea lies to the west. The Bay of Bengal borders to the east. The Indian Ocean lies to the south. India's northern land border is shared with Pakistan and Nepal. Bhutan, Bangladesh, Myanmar, and China lie to the northeast.

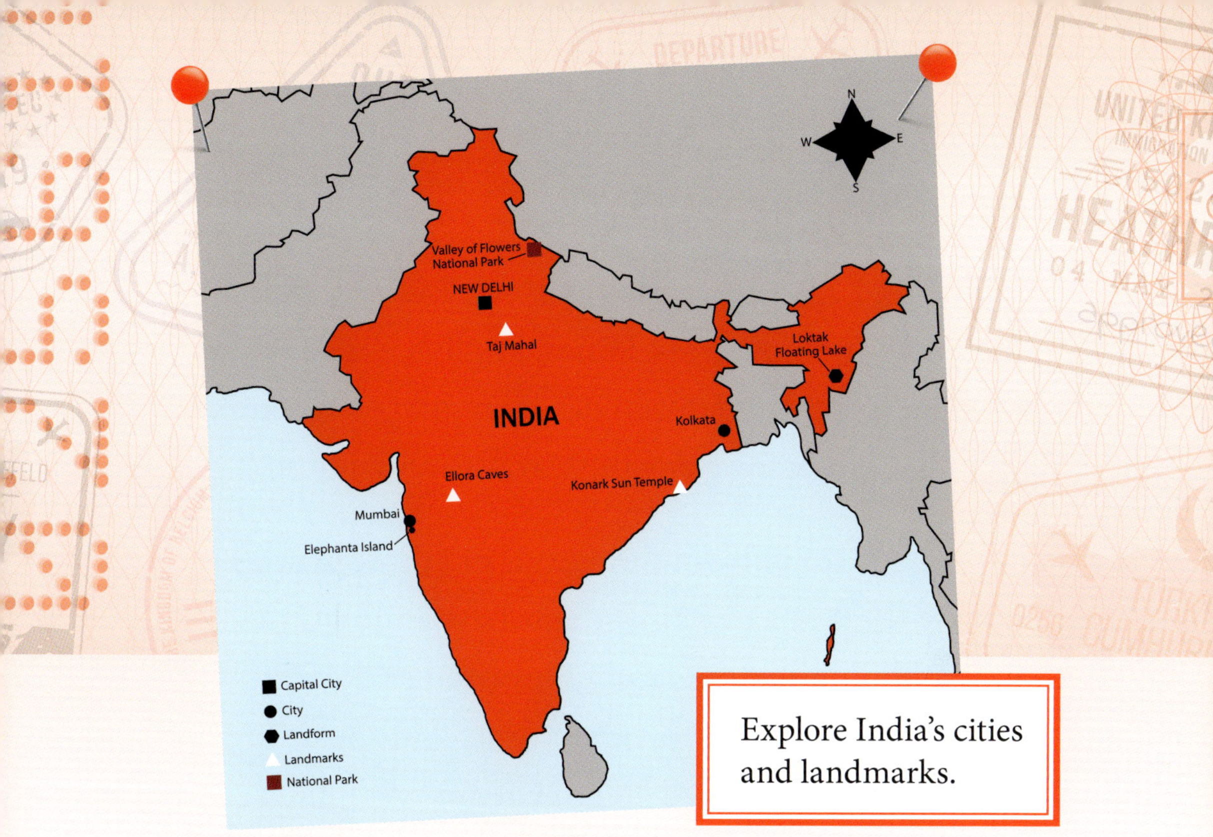

Explore India's cities and landmarks.

India has a varied landscape. The Himalaya Mountains are found in the north. The northwest region is desert. The southern region is mostly flat. Low mountains border the coasts. Many rivers run through the country. They include the Indus River, from which India gets its name.

Heavy rainfalls called monsoons control India's **climate**. They change the wind direction. Spring is usually hot and dry. Summers are hot and wet. India receives about 8 to 12 inches (20 to 30 centimeters) of rain from summer monsoons. Winters are cool and dry.

THE INDIAN PEOPLE

Around 1.4 billion people live in India. Nearly half of all Indians speak Hindi. English is also widely spoken. Nearly two dozen other languages are spoken in India, including Bengali, Marathi, and Tamil.

Indians come from thousands of ethnic groups. Nearly three out of four Indians have Indo-Aryan roots. Their **ancestors** were European and Asian. Many Indians have Dravidian roots and speak Dravidian languages. The Dravidians were **native** to India and arrived before the Indo-Aryans.

People shop at street markets in India.

FACT FILE

OFFICIAL NAME:	REPUBLIC OF INDIA
POPULATION:	1,409,128,296
LAND AREA:	1,269,219 SQ. MI. (3,287,263 SQ KM)
CAPITAL:	NEW DELHI
MONEY:	INDIAN RUPEE
GOVERNMENT:	FEDERAL PARLIAMENTARY REPUBLIC
LANGUAGE:	ENGLISH, HINDI

GEOGRAPHY: India is located in Asia. The Arabian Sea lies to the west, and the Bay of Bengal lies to the east. The Indian Ocean lies to the south. Pakistan is in the northwest. Nepal, Bhutan, Bangladesh, Myanmar, and China border to the northeast.

NATURAL RESOURCES: sugarcane, rice, wheat, iron ore

CHAPTER TWO

HISTORY OF INDIA

Hunter-gatherers first arrived in India about 30,000 years ago during the Stone Age. By 6500 BCE, new settlers were growing barley and wheat. They were also raising livestock, including cattle, sheep, and goats. Between 5000 and 2000 BCE, **urban** settlements spread out in the region. They traded with each other and outside civilizations across the Asian continent. These settlers also used early forms of written communication. They etched and stamped symbols and patterns in clay.

Around 2600 BCE, many ethnic groups came together. They formed the Indus **civilization**. These people had a common culture and lived in the Indus River Valley. They raised animals and grew crops such as rice and dates. The Indus people also made jewelry from gold, silver, and copper. They were skilled at pottery. Between 2000 and 1750 BCE, unknown invaders ended the Indus civilization by destroying the main cities in battle.

Archaeologists uncovered remains belonging to the Indus Valley civilization at an excavation site in Baghpat, India.

THE ARYANS ARRIVE

Between 1500 and 1200 BCE, the Aryan people invaded the region. They spoke many Indo-European languages and likely came from modern-day Kazakhstan. The Aryans were skilled at farming and crafts. They followed spiritual traditions and texts called Vedas that formed the roots of the Hindu religion.

MUSLIM RULE

Muslims first arrived in India around 700 CE. They followed the religion of Islam and came from Turkey and central Asia. Many rulers held power in different regions at once. In 1206, a centralized kingdom with one ruler was set up in Delhi. But small regional kingdoms remained all over India.

In 1526, the Mughal Empire took over northern India. It slowly defeated smaller kingdoms across the land with the skilled war tactics and leadership of its ruler, Babur. By the 1600s, the empire ruled over most of India.

The Lodi Empire used nearly 1,000 war elephants to fight against the Mughal Empire in The First Battle of Panipat in 1526.

During this time, Europeans from several countries settled in India. They competed to trade with the locals. India offered many valuable resources that were scarce in Europe, such as spices, medicines, textiles, and metals. In exchange, Europeans offered Indians gold and silver.

THE ROAD TO INDEPENDENCE

The Mughal Empire's power weakened in the 1700s. Around that time, the British East India Company was becoming a powerful force in world trade. It wanted to take over Bengal, India's richest province, to ensure Britain's rule. In 1757, the British military defeated the Bengal military in the Battle of Plassey. A British governor was appointed to rule over Bengal. The British government gained political and economic control of most of India.

The Indian people were angered by the British East India Company's control. Heavy taxation made many Indians poor. In 1857, Indian soldiers and citizens fought back in a war for independence. After a bloody battle, they lost to the British. But the British government was unhappy with the East India Company's lack of control over the Indians. The company was shut down within a year, and the British government began direct rule over India.

By 1885, many Indian people had lost jobs, paid high taxes, and starved during times when food was scarce. They created the Indian National Congress and chose Mahatma Gandhi as their leader.

TIMELINE OF INDIAN HISTORY

ABOUT 6500 BCE: The first settlers arrive in modern-day India.

ABOUT 2600 BCE: The Indus civilization settles in the region.

1500 BCE: Aryan invaders bring different traditions, governments, and languages to India.

321 BCE: The Mauryan Empire becomes the first to unite the region.

700 CE: The first Muslims arrive in India.

1526: The Mughal Empire takes over India.

1858: India falls under British rule after failed protests.

1920: Mahatma Gandhi encourages Indians to protest peacefully against the British.

1947: India becomes independent, splitting its land into the countries of India and Pakistan.

1948: India and Pakistan fight the first of several wars over territory.

2008: India launches its first lunar mission.

2014: India strikes a major economic deal with China.

In 1920, Gandhi encouraged Indians to resist British power peacefully. For more than 20 years, Indians protested and refused to buy British goods. In 1947, India became independent. Some of its land became the country of Pakistan. Religious, ethnic, and political problems still trouble the country. A growing population and poverty remain issues. But over time, India has become a strong **democracy** with a powerful **economy**.

CHAPTER THREE

EXPLORE INDIA

India has many interesting cities and historic sites. **Relics** of its many cultures, both past and present, can be found all over the country.

MODERN CITIES

New Delhi is the capital of India. Markets sell colorful fabrics, crafts, and foods. Visitors can see the massive Red Fort. The red, sandstone palace was built by the Mughal Empire. The nearby Jama Masjid is the largest **mosque** in the city. It can welcome 25,000 visitors at once.

Jama Masjid is Arabic for "Friday mosque." Many Muslims gather here on Fridays for communal prayer.

Mumbai is another bustling city. Gold and silver jewelry are found at the Zaveri Bazaar.

Elephanta Island has a maze of rock temples. People can admire its large statues, **shrines**, and courtyards.

Kolkata is home to the Botanical Gardens. More than 12,000 plant species are found there. Visitors can ride boats in its lakes with giant water lily pads. The Indian Museum features ancient sculptures from the Indus Valley civilization.

Giant lilies float in a lake at a botanical garden in Kolkata.

NATURAL WONDERS

India is a place of many natural wonders. Keibul Lamjao National Park is located in northeastern India. Loktak Lake is found there. This lake has many small, floating islands made of plants and soil. Many kinds of birds, butterflies, and fish live at the park. The endangered Sangai deer roams the land.

Valley of Flowers National Park lies in the western Himalayas. More than 600 plant and flower species grow in this area. Glaciers and waterfalls surround the park.

Pink persicaria affinis are one of the flowers that grow in the Valley of Flowers National Park.

The Taj Mahal is located in a Mughal garden. Its construction took more than 20 years to complete.

MONUMENTS

The Taj Mahal is one of India's most famous monuments. It is located in northern India. It was completed in 1648. The ruler Shah Jahan had it built as a tomb for his wife. The building is carved from white marble and decorated with colorful gemstones.

FACT

Sangai deer have adapted to walking on the moving islands. They feed on the plants that grow on the islands. Scientists think there are fewer than 1,000 of these animals in the wild.

CHAPTER FOUR

DAILY LIFE

One out of three Indians live in urban areas. Some residents live in houses or apartments. Poorer residents often live in huts or shanties in overcrowded areas called slums. They may live in makeshift homes made from mud or bricks with a cement or tin roof. Cars, buses, and trains offer transportation.

Most Indians live in villages. Many live in one-story mud homes. Wealthier Indians live in larger homes made of brick or stone. Rural residents often get around on foot or by bus.

People live in homes on the banks of the Ganges River.

Many Indians work on farms that raise sugarcane, tea, coffee, and spices. They may also raise cattle. A large number of Indians work in tourism. Transportation and technology jobs are also common. A smaller number of Indians work in factories or mines.

FACT

Cattle are sacred animals in the Hindu religion. For this reason, many Indians do not eat meat from cattle. They drink their milk and use them as work animals.

THE CASTE SYSTEM

Indians are born into one of four social classes called castes. The top caste contains Hindu priests and scholars. The next caste contains rulers and military leaders. The third caste is for merchants and farmers. The last caste contains servants, workers, and artisans. A person's caste is based on their family, wealth, and job. Many aspects of Indian life, including diet, social customs, and marriage are determined by a person's caste.

TRADITIONS AND FAMILY

Indian families are very close. Many generations may live in one house. Family members often share costs. They make major decisions together, such as arranging marriages and moving homes.

About 75 percent of Indians follow the Hindu religion. A large number of people are Muslim. Smaller groups are Buddhist, Jain, Christian, or Sikh.

INDIAN WEDDINGS

Indian weddings are often big celebrations that take place over several days. Their traditions vary by family, caste, and religion. Some marriages are arranged. Family members help match their grown children with someone from the same caste and religion. But love marriages, or marriages that are not arranged, are becoming more common. Couples sometimes marry outside their religion or caste.

Time with family is very important to many Indians.

Indian clothing varies by region, caste, and religion. Many men, especially in rural areas, wear loose-fitting pants with no shirt. Men in urban areas and of the Muslim and Sikh religions often wear fitted shirts and pants. Most women in India wear a sari. It is a colorful cotton or silk garment wrapped around the body. Some women wear pants with a sari, while others wear skirts.

INDIAN FOOD

Rice, bread, and vegetables are common in Indian meals. But dishes vary by region. In southern India, breakfast may include steamed rice cakes called idli. They are served with lentil stew. In northern India, round breads called bhature are eaten with spicy chickpea curry.

Khichdi is a dish eaten all over India. It is made of rice, lentils, and spices. Common meat dishes include vindaloo pork made with chiles and spices. Lamb korma is a popular stew cooked in spices and yogurt. Palak paneer is a cheese dish served in spinach sauce. Desserts include rice pudding and cashew fudge candy. Fried sweets called jalebi are enjoyed at celebrations.

Palak paneer

NANKHATAI

Nankhatai are butter cookies that are easy to make. These popular cookies have been enjoyed in India for hundreds of years.

Ingredients

- 1 cup all-purpose or wheat flour
- ½ cup chickpea flour
- ½ teaspoon cardamom
- ¼ teaspoon nutmeg
- ½ teaspoon baking powder
- ½ cup salted butter at room temperature
- ⅓ cup sweetened condensed milk
- ½ teaspoon vanilla extract
- chopped almonds (optional)

Directions

1. Preheat the oven to 350 degrees Fahrenheit (177 degrees Celsius).
2. Mix the flours, cardamom, nutmeg, and baking powder in a large mixing bowl.
3. Add in the butter, milk, and vanilla.
4. Mix all the ingredients with a whisk or electric mixer until they become a soft dough.
5. Using your hands, divide the dough into about a dozen small balls. Flatten each ball slightly to make a cookie shape.
6. Arrange the cookies on a greased baking tray and bake for around 12 minutes. The cookies should have brown edges.
7. Let the cookies cool for a few minutes on a cooling rack. Then sprinkle chopped almonds on them if you would like.

CHAPTER FIVE

HOLIDAYS AND CELEBRATIONS

Indians celebrate many holidays. Diwali is called the festival of lights. It is celebrated by Hindus, Sikhs, and Jains. Diwali is celebrated in October or November over five days. Friends and family offer gifts, enjoy feasts, and light lamps and fireworks.

Holi is a Hindu festival celebrated in northern India. It is held at the start of spring. It is often called the festival of colors. People throw colored powders at each other. They sing, dance, and eat together. Sometimes bonfires are lit at night.

The colored powder people throw during Holi is called gulal. The colors used represent many meanings for Hindus.

Buddhists celebrate Vesak in the spring or summer. This holiday celebrates the life of Buddha, the teacher of Buddhism. Muslims celebrate holidays including Eid-al Fitr. It marks the end of the holy month of Ramadan. Muslims celebrate by enjoying feasts.

NATIONAL HOLIDAYS

Indians celebrate national holidays as well. August 15 is Independence Day. Indians dress in the flag colors of dark orange, white, and green and attend ceremonies. They celebrate their independence from the British. Gandhi Jayanti is on October 2nd. Indians celebrate Mahatma Gandhi's birthday. They pray and honor the man who taught them peace over violence.

CHAPTER SIX

SPORTS AND RECREATION

Music and dance are important to Indian culture. Hindustani music is played in the north. It features rhythmic music made with string and percussion instruments. A singer sometimes sings along. In the south, vocal music is more popular. Instruments such as the violin and the mridangam, a double-sided drum, mimic a singer's sounds.

Dance styles are regional and often reflect religious traditions. One popular dance is bhangra from the Punjab region. Dancers do a lively dance of kicks and leaps set to rhythmic music.

Bhangra was originally a traditional dance performed at festivals celebrating Vaisakhi.

FACT

The Indian film industry, called Bollywood, makes more than 1,000 movies per year. The films often feature lively dances performed in colorful costumes.

Virat Kohli and Shubman Gill of India compete in the ICC Men's Cricket World Cup 2023 between India and Sri Lanka at Wankhede stadium.

Many Indians also enjoy games and sports. Cricket is very popular throughout India. The Indian team has competed in World Cup games. Kabaddi is an ancient game still played today. It combines rugby and wrestling. Kho-kho is a kind of tag game. Professional players compete nationally on teams.

India is a land of many wonders. From lively music and delicious dishes to religious traditions, India is a country where the ancient past meets the present.

LAGORI

Lagori is a popular children's game from southern India. Some versions use wooden blocks instead of stones.

What You Need:

- two teams with three players each
- seven medium-sized stones, about 6 to 8 inches (15 to 20 cm) long
- a coin
- a rubber or bouncy ball

What You Do:

1. Stack the stones in an open playing area. Flip a coin to decide which team goes first.
2. The starting team takes the ball and stands about 10 feet (3 meters) away. One player on that team tries to throw the ball at the stones and topple all of them. Each team gets nine chances, with each player getting three chances.
3. If the starting team does not topple all the stones after nine chances, the other team gets a turn.
4. As soon as a team topples all the stones, this team must try to stack them back.
5. As they stack, the opposite team tries to hit the stacking team members with the ball by throwing it. The opposite team can pass the ball to each other but cannot run with it.
6. If the stacking team stacks all the stones without anyone getting hit, this team gets a point, and they get a new turn. If the throwing team hits any stacking team player, the throwing team gets a point. They get to play next.
7. The team that earns 10 points first wins the game.

GLOSSARY

ancestor (AN-ses-tur)
a member from a person's family who lived a long time ago

civilization (sih-vuh-ly-ZAY-shun)
a highly developed and organized society

climate (KLY-muht)
weather in a specific place over a period of time

culture (KUL-chur)
a people's way of life, ideas, art, customs, and traditions

democracy (deh-MAH-cruh-see)
a form of government in which the citizens can choose their leaders

economy (eh-KON-uh-mee)
the way money is made and spent

hunter-gatherers (HUNT-ur-GATH-ur-urs)
people who hunt, fish, and search for food rather than farming or raising animals

mosque (MOSK)
a building where Muslims gather together to worship

native (NAY-tiv)
belonging to a specific place by birth

relics (REH-liks)
traces of customs or beliefs left from the past

shrine (SHRINE)
a place where saints or gods are worshipped

urban (UR-buhn)
related to cities and city life

READ MORE

Green, Sara. *Taj Mahal*. Minneapolis, MN: Bellwether Media, 2021.

Hyde, Natalie. *Focus on India*. New York, NY: Crabtree Publishing, 2025.

Murray, Julie. *India*. Minneapolis, MN: ABDO Publishing, 2026.

INTERNET SITES

BBC Bitesize: What Is Holi?
bbc.co.uk/bitesize/articles/z4qqy9q

National Geographic Kids: Diwali: Festival of Lights
kids.nationalgeographic.com/pages/article/diwali

National Geographic Kids: India
kids.nationalgeographic.com/geography/countries/article/india

INDEX

ABOUT THE AUTHOR

Golriz Golkar is the author of more than 70 books for children. Inspired by her work as an elementary school teacher, she loves to write the kinds of books that children are excited to read. Golriz holds a B.A. in American literature and culture from UCLA and a master's degree in education from the Harvard Graduate School of Education. Golriz lives in France with her husband and young daughter, and they all love reading together.

SELECT BOOKS IN THIS SERIES

YOUR PASSPORT TO AUSTRALIA
YOUR PASSPORT TO BRAZIL
YOUR PASSPORT TO CUBA
YOUR PASSPORT TO EGYPT
YOUR PASSPORT TO ENGLAND
YOUR PASSPORT TO GERMANY
YOUR PASSPORT TO JAPAN
YOUR PASSPORT TO MEXICO
YOUR PASSPORT TO PORTUGAL
YOUR PASSPORT TO SAUDI ARABIA